MW00910778

Buddy BOOKS
Prehistoric Animals

Giant Rhino

ABDO
Publishing Company

A Buddy Book
by
Michael P. Goecke

VISIT US AT
www.abdopub.com

Published by Buddy Books, an imprint of ABDO Publishing Company, 4940 Viking Drive, Edina, Minnesota 55435. Copyright © 2003 by Abdo Consulting Group, Inc. International copyrights reserved in all countries. No part of this book may be reproduced in any form without written permission from the publisher.

Printed in the United States.

Edited by: Christy DeVillier
Contributing Editor: Matt Ray
Graphic Design: Deborah Coldiron
Image Research: Deborah Coldiron
Illustrations: Deborah Coldiron, Denise Esner
Photographs: Corbis, Hulton Archives, Steve McHugh, Photodisc

Library of Congress Cataloging-in-Publication Data

Goecke, Michael P., 1968-
     Giant rhino / Michael P. Goecke.
         p. cm. — (Prehistoric animals. Set I)
     Includes index.
     Summary: Introduces the physical characteristics, habitat, and behavior of a prehistoric relative of the modern-day rhinoceros.
     Contents: Prehistoric animals — Giant rhino — What did it look like? — Discovery — Why so big? — When did it live and where? — Rhinoceros — How did it disappear?
     ISBN 1-57765-969-4
     1. Indricotherium—Juvenile literature. 2. Paleontology—Oligocene—Juvenile literature. [1. Indricotherium. 2. Rhinoceroses, Fossil. 3. Prehistoric animals. 4. Paleontology.] I. Title.

QE882.U6 G256 2003
569'.668—dc21

                                                                                    2002028196

Table of Contents

Prehistoric Animals

Millions of years ago, there were no cities. There were no buildings, cars, or people. Dinosaurs and other prehistoric animals roamed the earth.

Dinosaurs died out about 65 million years ago. Mammals became common after the dinosaurs. Some prehistoric mammals were saber-toothed cats, mammoths, and giant rhinos.

Prehistoric Animals

The Giant Rhino

Indricotherium
(in-DRIK-oh-THEE-ree-um)

The *Indricotherium* was a prehistoric rhino. It was one of the biggest land mammals that ever lived. The *Indricotherium* is related to today's rhinos. Some people call it the giant rhino.

Giant rhinos lived in Asia for thousands of years. Their fossils have been found in Pakistan, Mongolia, and China.

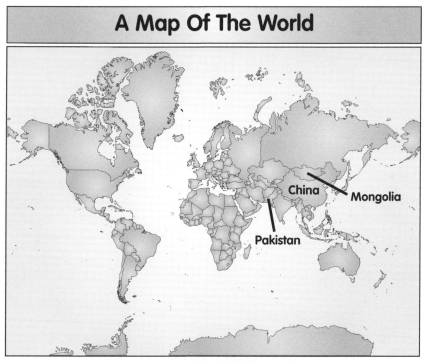

A Map Of The World

Giant rhino fossils have been found in Pakistan, Mongolia, and China.

The giant rhino was about four times bigger than today's rhinos. It grew to become about 15 feet (5 m) tall. An adult weighed about 17 tons (15 t). This giant mammal was about 26 feet (8 m) long.

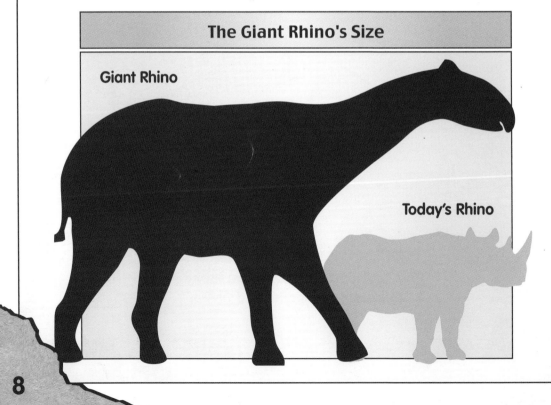

The Giant Rhino's Size

Giant Rhino

Today's Rhino

The giant rhino was one of the biggest land mammals.

The giant rhino had a long neck. It could reach the tops of 20 foot (6 m) trees.

The giant rhino's head was about four feet (one m) long. Unlike today's rhinos, the giant rhino had no horn on its head.

The giant rhino walked on four thick legs. Each foot had three toes. Each toe had a hard covering. This covering is called a hoof. Today's rhinos have hoofed feet, too.

Giant rhinos were plant eaters. Like giraffes, they probably ate leaves from treetops. Giant rhinos had four big teeth for chewing food.

The giant rhino had a long neck like today's giraffes.

11

Some scientists believe giant rhinos lived in groups called herds. Others believe they lived like today's rhinos. Today's adult rhinos commonly live alone.

Today's rhinos mostly live alone.

Scientists believe that it is easier for larger animals to go without food and water. Some animals can last days without eating or drinking.

The giant rhino was a very large animal. So maybe it could last for days between meals, too.

13

Adult giant rhinos were probably safe from predators. But *Hyaenodons* may have hunted their young. *Hyaenodons* were dog-like meat eaters.

Hyaenodons (hy-EE-noh-donz) were deadly predators.

Hyaenodons

Hyaenodons were predators. They could run fast and bite hard. Some *Hyaenodons* were as small as foxes. Others were as big as today's rhinos.

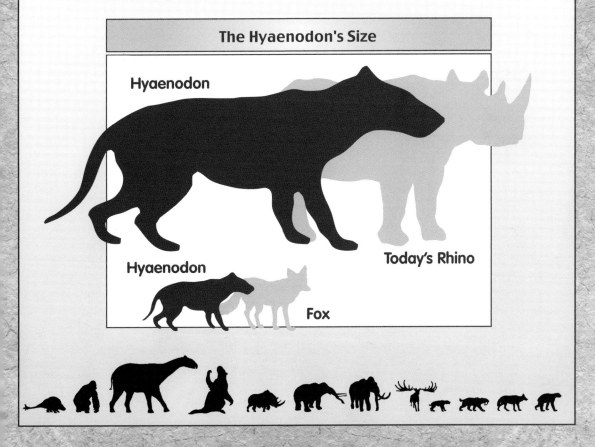

The Hyaenodon's Size

Hyaenodon

Today's Rhino

Hyaenodon

Fox

Giant Rhino's World

Scientists have names for important time periods in Earth's history. The giant rhino lived during a time called the Oligocene.

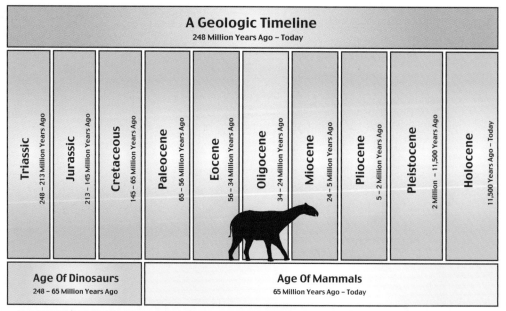

A Geologic Timeline
248 Million Years Ago – Today

| Triassic 248 – 213 Million Years Ago | Jurassic 213 – 145 Million Years Ago | Cretaceous 145 – 65 Million Years Ago | Paleocene 65 – 56 Million Years Ago | Eocene 56 – 34 Million Years Ago | Oligocene 34 – 24 Million Years Ago | Miocene 24 – 5 Million Years Ago | Pliocene 5 – 2 Million Years Ago | Pleistocene 2 Million – 11,500 Years Ago | Holocene 11,500 Years Ago – Today |

Age Of Dinosaurs
248 – 65 Million Years Ago

Age Of Mammals
65 Million Years Ago – Today

The giant rhino lived between 30 and 25 million years ago.

The world's climate became cooler during the Oligocene. A giant sheet of ice covered the South Pole. The seas had less water. Woodlands were common.

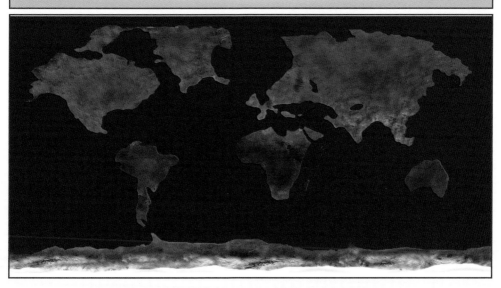

The Oligocene World

Woodlands were common during the Oligocene.

17

Giant rhinos lived among many other plant-eating mammals. There were mastodon elephants, deer, cattle, horses, camels, and prehistoric pigs. The first dogs and cats appeared at the end of the Oligocene.

Grasslands became common at the end of the Oligocene. These grasslands probably had few trees for giant rhinos to eat. This may be why giant rhinos died out.

Some animals, such as today's lions, are well-suited to living on grasslands.

Exciting Discovery

Why do scientists know so much about prehistoric life? They study fossils. A fossil can be a bone or a footprint. Any trace of life from long ago is a fossil.

Roy Chapman Andrews was a fossil hunter. In 1922, he began looking for giant rhino fossils in Mongolia. At that time, there were very few giant rhino fossils.

A giant rhino tooth fossil.

One day, Andrews's driver noticed a big jawbone in the ground. This jawbone was a fossil. It belonged to a prehistoric giant rhino. Andrews found the giant rhino's skull and many more of its bones.

Roy Chapman Andrews

Bandits almost stole Andrews's giant rhino fossils. But he got away from them. Andrews shipped the fossils to the New York Museum of Natural History. Thanks to Roy Chapman Andrews, scientists have learned a lot about the giant rhino.

Important Words

climate the weather of a place over time.

fossil remains of very old animals and plants commonly found in the ground. A fossil can be a bone, a footprint, or any trace of life.

mammal most living things that belong to this special group have hair, give birth to live babies, and make milk to feed their babies.

Oligocene a period of time that began about 34 million years ago and lasted about 10 million years.

predator an animal that hunts and eats other animals.

prehistoric describes anything that was around more than 5,500 years ago.

Web Sites

To learn more about the giant rhino, visit ABDO Publishing Company on the World Wide Web. Web sites about the giant rhino are featured on our Book Links page. These links are routinely monitored and updated to provide the most current information available.

www.abdopub.com

23

24